W9-BMN-339

This document is geared towards providing exact and reliable information in regards to the topic and issue covered. The publication is sold with the idea that the publisher is not required to render accounting, officially permitted, or otherwise, qualified services. If advice is necessary, legal or professional, a practiced individual in the profession should be ordered.

Under no circumstance will any legal responsibility or blame be held against the publisher for any reparation, damages, or monetary loss due to the information herein, either directly or indirectly.

Legal Notice:

Disclaimer Notice:

Please note the information contained within this document is for educational and entertainment purposes only. Every attempt has been made to provide accurate, up to date and reliable complete information. No warranties of any kind are expressed or implied. Readers acknowledge that the author is not engaging in the rendering of legal, financial, medical or professional advice. The content of this book has been derived from various sources. Please consult a licensed professional before attempting any techniques outlined in this book.

By reading this document, the reader agrees that under no circumstances are is the author responsible for any loses, direct or indirect, which are incurred as a result the use of information contained within this document, including, but not limited to, —errors, omissions, or inaccuracies.

Table of Contents

Introduction

Chapter 1 - Why Meal Prepping?

What Is Meal Prepping?

When we meal prep we prepare all or some of our meals for the week, in advance. Meal prepping is a popular concept, that you have probably seen on social media or heard about on talk shows or your local news. Meal prepping is a great way to provide yourself with the most delicious, nutritious, and healthy foods without any processed ingredients.

The hectic routines of our daily lives make meal prepping an effective and convenient way to stick to a diet or lifestyle while also saving time and money. It's a medium to have nutritious, tasty food available no matter what challenges daily life throws at you. Meal prepping can also prevent the last minute decisions we make when we are hungry that lead to the dangers of processed, canned and packaged foods.

Meal prepping can mean different things, depending on your personal needs. It can mean preparing a bunch of vegetables for the coming week, or making several, different meals for work lunches, or even preparing larger quantities of easy to re-heat meals and freezing them for later use. You will have to take some time out of your schedule for washing, chopping, and packing but in the end the rewards are worth it. Prepare dinners and lunches by roasting vegetables in advance, cook large quantity of your lean meats and then pack them in a quick grab and go containers for an easy approach to dinner or lunch. You can also prepare a bit extra of a meal you are already making but so that you have a quick to go meal for those days when you are too tired or busy to cook.

Consider these tips:

- Prepare and freeze fruits and yogurt into smoothies for a week to have a quick nutritious breakfast.

- Taco meats, fajita fillings, soups, breakfast burritos, and egg muffins are easy, bulk foods that work beautifully for meal prepping.
- Chop your vegetables in advance.
- Preparing lean proteins on the weekends and pack up in grab and go containers to make your lunches during the week a breeze.

Chapter 2 - The Basics of Meal Planning:

Meal planning is the core foundation of successful meal prepping. Meal planning allows you to create your meals for the upcoming week before prepping them. Meal planning is the first step you can take to ensure your success in following a balanced, nutritious, healthy and delicious diet. It takes the guess work out of grocery shopping, and ensures you have all of the ingredients you need before you start your prep work.

What Is The Difference Between Meal Planning And Meal Prepping?

Meal prepping and meal planning work together to ensure the effectiveness of your plan. Meal planning answers your questions about what to have for each meal, while meal prepping is the act of preparing those meals. Without meal planning, meal prepping would be more complex and harder to adopt. Meal prepping is the practical execution of your meal planning it allows you to plot out your meals in advance, get the required ingredients for the recipes, and organize your week instead of being stymied by the daily decisions regarding what you will eat.

Never planned a meal in your life? Not sure how to start? There are several tips and tricks you can find on the internet. Social media sites like Pinterest, are fantastic resources, filled with recipes and ideas to help get you started on your meal planning adventure.

Chapter 3 - 4 Reasons Why You Should Meal Prep on Keto:

There are several reasons why you should use meal prepping while following a ketogenic diet plan or lifestyle.

1. The keto requires your meals follow a very specific break down of the calories you consume in each meal. (i.e. 5% carbohydrates, 20% proteins and 75% fats).
2. Planning for an entire week can help alleviate the stress of preparing each meal individually.
3. It saves time, money, and energy. Although following a keto diet plan is not expensive on its face. You could find yourself spending extra time and money repeatedly making trips to the grocery store, wasting unused food or getting takeout. Meal prepping prevents these common pitfalls.
4. Meal prepping ensures that your time is not spend slaving in the kitchen, freeing you up to spend more time with the people you care about and doing the activities you enjoy.

How to Start Keto Meal Prepping Today?

The most successful meal prepping is simple. Don't over complicate your meals. Choose simple, easy to follow recipes that include whole, nutritious foods that you like.

For example, in the beginning avoid recipes which you haven't previously made. In the beginning, go for recipes which you have prepared previously and know well. Then as you become comfortable with meal prepping, get more adventurous. Go for new recipes and innovative ideas as soon as you start getting adjusted to the process. Meal prepping is a key to success when doing any keto diet. To start efficiently meal prepping on your keto plan, follow try the following simple steps:

1. **Choose a Prep Day:**

    Start with selecting a specific day and time to prepare your meals. This is the initial step of any meal prepping. Sunday is commonly preferred for this purpose as it is the day before the dreaded Monday work week begins, but any day that works for you is a good day to start. In the beginning consider prepping your meals for 2-3 days. You can always increase your meal amounts later. Some experienced meal prepping devotees divide their meal prepping days for a week into half i.e. Sunday and Wednesday.

2. Choose Your Meals:

Which recipe to follow and the amount to be prepared is a vital question you will want to answer before starting any meal prep. You may preferably go for dinners first, or you may opt for prepping breakfasts and lunches first. Choose various recipes for different meal times.

3. Use the Proper Jars & Containers:

Before you start any of your meal prepping make sure you have the proper storage containers and jars for the food you have prepped. Food storage can determine the success and how efficient your meal prepping is. Air tight jars and containers should be the preferred containers for meal prepping. These containers help to maintain the freshness of your food. They also typically freeze well. Don't forget a good marker to label your containers properly. The following jars and containers are best suited for meal prepping:

- Stackable
- Freezer Safe
- Microwaveable
- Reusable
- Dishwasher Safe
- Freezer Safe
- BPA Free

Chapter 4 - Equipments Needed For Meal Prepping

Aside from the proper storage containers you shouldn't need to purchase anything extra to successfully meal prep for your keto diet. However, there are some products out there that can make meal prepping easier for you. Check out the list below for some ideas:

1. **Quirky Cutting Board with Storage Containers:**

   A good chopping block or cutting board can be a prepper's dream. Finding something similar to the Quirky Mocubu Cutting Board, which includes storage containers in various sizes that attach right to it can allow you to see the portions you are creating. Simply chop and store your veggies into any of three drawers below the board and there you go, no worries until the next recipe!

2. **Black and Decker Three-Cup Electric Food Chopper:**

   The Black and Decker chopper will do all the dicing for you. Don't like to chop? Simply toss your vegetables into it and let the machine do the work. This can save you time in the next steps of your recipes.

3. **New Star Heavy Duty Three-Slice Egg Slicer:**

   It doesn't matter if you are cutting strawberries for a morning cereal, dicing mushroom for a dinner recipe ,or slicing eggs for a salad in your lunches, an egg slicer can come in super handy. The New Star Heavy Duty Three-Slice Egg Slicer is one option to help you do it all.

4. **Cuisinart Two-Speed Hand Blender:**

   Soups can be a dream for a beginning meal prepper. Cuisinart Two-Speed Hand Blender can be very useful for recipes which need puréeing. This is a single handed immersion blender perfect for soups and other large pot blending.

5. **Silpat Non-stick Silicone Baking Sheet:**

There could be a lot of roasted veggies in your recipes if you are meal prepping, and we encourage it. The more roasted veggies the better. You can go eco and money friendly by getting something similar to the Silpat Non-stick Silicone Baking Sheet. A reusable baking sheet will allow you to use less parchment paper. Saving time and money.

6. **Wilton Silicone Muffin Pan:**

   So many great keto recipes can be made as muffins. A stellar muffin tin is required to make your prepping life easier. The Wilton Silicone Muffin Pan is stain resistant and easy to wash.

7. **Instant Pot Pressure Cooker:**

   The Instant Pot is a revolution of its own. There are thousands of recipes online, almost all of them ideal for meal prepping. It can cook anything ranging from oatmeal, stew, meat, preparing yogurt and much more in so much less time than a typical slow cooker. A good instant pot could be the backbone of any successful prepper.

8. **Bentgo Stackable Lunch Box:**

   We have talked about the importance of the right storage containers for prepped grab and go meals. The Bengto Stackable Lunch Box is one such container. These storage boxes are manufactured with plastic flatware which is built-in, making them perfect for the busy work day lunch.

21-Day Meal Plan

Day 1

Breakfast: Berry Blast Smoothie

Serves: 2

Preparation Time: 10 minutes

Ingredients:

- ½ cup fresh strawberries
- ½ cup fresh blueberries
- 2 cups fresh spinach
- 3-4 drops liquid stevia
- 1½ cups unsweetened almond milk

Instructions:

1) In a high-speed blender, add all ingredients and pulse until smooth.
2) Transfer into 2 serving glasses and serve immediately.

Meal Prep Tip: In 2 containers, divide all ingredients except almond milk and stevia. Cover and store in freezer for about 2-3 days. Just before serving, remove containers from freezer and transfer into a blender with almond milk and stevia and pulse until smooth.

Nutrition Information:

Calories per serving: 69; Carbohydrates: 10.6g; Protein: 2.1g; Fat: 3g; Sugar: 5.5g; Sodium: 704mg; Fiber: 3g

Lunch: 2 Veggies Platter

Serves: 4

Cooking Time: 16 minutes

Preparation Time: 15 minutes

Ingredients:

- 2 tablespoons butter
- 2 tablespoons onion, minced
- ½ teaspoon garlic, minced
- 1 (8-ounce) package white mushrooms, sliced
- Pinch of salt
- 1 cup frozen green beans

Instructions:

1) In a large skillet, melt butter over medium heat.
2) Sauté onion and garlic for about 1 minute.
3) Add mushrooms and cook for 5 minutes.
4) Stir in green beans and cook for 8-10 minutes more.
5) Serve hot.

Meal Prep Tip: Transfer the 2 Veggies Platter in a large bowl and set aside to cool completely. Divide the mixture into 4 containers evenly. Cover the containers and refrigerate for about 2 days. Reheat in the microwave before serving.

Nutrition Information:

Calories per serving: 74; Carbohydrates: 4.4g; Protein: 2.4g; Fat: 6g; Sugar: 1.6g; Sodium: 219mg; Fiber: 1.6g

Dinner: Deliciously Spicy Turkey

Serves: 6

Cooking Time: 18 minutes

Preparation Time: 20 minutes

Ingredients for Spice Blend:

- 1 teaspoon xanthan gum
- 2 teaspoons ground coriander
- 1 teaspoon ground cumin
- 1/8 teaspoon ground cloves
- 1/8 teaspoon ground cinnamon
- 1/8 teaspoon ground turmeric
- 1/8 teaspoon cayenne pepper
- Salt and freshly ground black pepper, to taste

Ingredients for Turkey:

- 1¼ pounds ground turkey
- 1 small yellow onion, sliced
- 2 teaspoons fresh ginger, minced
- 2 teaspoons garlic, minced
- 1 medium tomato, chopped
- ½ cup water
- ½ cup unsweetened coconut milk
- 2 tablespoons fresh cilantro, chopped

Instructions:

1) For spice blend: in a bowl, mix together all ingredients and set aside.
2) Heat a nonstick skillet over medium-high heat and cook turkey, onion, ginger and garlic for about 5-6 minutes or until browned.
3) Remove any excess fat from skillet.

4) Add spice blend and cook for about 2 minutes.

5) Stir in remaining ingredients except cilantro and bring to a gentle boil.

6) Reduce the heat to medium-low and simmer for about 10 minutes.

7) Stir in cilantro and serve immediately.

Meal Prep Tip: Remove the turkey mixture from heat and set aside to cool completely. In 6 containers, divide the turkey mixture evenly and refrigerate for about 2 days. Reheat in microwave before serving.

Nutrition Information:

Calories per serving: 246; Carbohydrates: 4.6g; Protein:.26.8g; Fat: 15.3g; Sugar: 1.7g; Sodium: 1466mg; Fiber: 1.7g

Day 2

Breakfast: Delish Pancakes

Serves: 2

Cooking Time: 12 minutes

Preparation Time: 15 minutes

Ingredients:

- 2 organic eggs
- 2-ounce cream cheese, softened
- ½ teaspoon ground cinnamon
- 1 packet stevia

Instructions:

1) In a blender, add all ingredients and pulse until smooth.
2) Set aside for about 2-3 minutes.
3) Heat a greased nonstick skillet over medium heat.
4) Add ¼ of the mixture.
5) Cook for about 2 minutes or until tops are bubbly.
6) Flip and cook for about 1 minute.
7) Repeat with the remaining mixture.

Meal Prep Tip: Store these cooled pancakes in a container by placing a piece of wax paper between each pancake. Refrigerate up to 4 days. Reheat in the microwave for about 1½-2 minutes.

Nutrition Information:

Calories per serving: 163; Carbohydrates: 2.6g; Protein: 7.7g; Fat: 14.3g; Sugar: 0.4g; Sodium: 146mg; Fiber: 0.3g

Lunch: Tangy Shrimp Salad

Serves: 12

Cooking Time: 3 minutes

Preparation Time: 15 minutes

Ingredients:

- 4 pounds large shrimp
- 1 lemon, quartered
- 3 cups celery stalks, chopped
- 1 yellow onion, chopped
- 2 cups mayonnaise
- 2 tablespoons balsamic vinegar
- 1 teaspoon Dijon mustard
- Salt and freshly ground black pepper, to taste

Instructions:

1) In a large pan of salted boiling water, add shrimp and lemon and cook for about 3 minutes.
2) Drain well and set aside to cool.
3) Then peel and devein the shrimps.
4) In a large bowl, add cooked shrimp and remaining ingredients.
5) Gently stir to combine.
6) Serve immediately.

Meal Prep Tip: In 12 containers, evenly divide Tangy Shrimp Salad. Refrigerate for about 1 day.

Nutrition Information:

Calories per serving: 342; Carbohydrates: 12g; Protein: 35.1g; Fat: 15.7g; Sugar: 3.3g; Sodium: 673mg; Fiber: 0.7g

Dinner: Greek Spinach Pie

Serves: 5

Cooking Time: 40 minutes

Preparation Time: 15 minutes

Ingredients:

- 2 tablespoons butter, divided
- 2 tablespoons yellow onion, chopped
- 1 (16-ounce) bag frozen chopped spinach, thawed and squeezed
- 1½ cups heavy cream
- 3 organic eggs
- ½ teaspoon ground nutmeg
- Salt and freshly ground black pepper, to taste
- ½ cup Swiss cheese, shredded

Instructions:

1) Preheat the oven to 375 degrees F. Grease a 9-inch pie dish.
2) In a large skillet, melt 1 tablespoon of butter over medium-high heat and sauté onion for about 4-5 minutes.
3) Add spinach and cook for 2-3 minutes or until all the liquid is absorbed.
4) In a bowl add cream, eggs, nutmeg, salt and black pepper. Beat until well combined.
5) Transfer the spinach mixture in the bottom of prepared pie dish, evenly. Top with the egg mixture.
6) Sprinkle with Swiss cheese evenly and top with the remaining butter in the shape of dots at many places.
7) Bake for about 25-30 minutes or until top becomes golden brown.
8) Remove from heat and set aside for about 5 minutes.
9) Cut evenly into 5 servings and serve.

Meal Prep Tip: Remove the pie from oven and set aside to cool completely. In 5 containers, divide the pie slices evenly and refrigerate for about 2 days. Reheat in microwave before serving.

Nutrition Information:

Calories per serving: 599; Carbohydrates: 8.2g; Protein:.11.6g; Fat: 59.5g; Sugar: 1.1g; Sodium: 243mg; Fiber: 2.2g

Day 3

Breakfast: No-Fail Omelet

Serves: 3

Cooking Time: 5 minutes

Preparation Time: 10 minutes

Ingredients:

- 6 large organic eggs
- 2 large organic egg yolks
- 2 tablespoons heavy whipping cream
- 1 tablespoon fresh parsley, chopped
- Salt and freshly ground black pepper, to taste
- 1½ tablespoons chilled butter, cubed and divided

Instructions:

1) In a bowl, add eggs, egg yolks, cream, parsley, salt and black pepper. Beat until frothy.
2) Set aside for about 15 minutes.
3) Add 1 tablespoon of butter into the egg mixture and set aside.
4) In an 8-inch nonstick skillet, melt ½ tablespoon of butter over low heat.
5) Add egg mixture and cook until set completely, scraping it off the bottom and the sides.
6) Remove from heat and set aside while covered for about 1-2 minutes.
7) With the spatula, slowly roll cooked eggs into an omelet.
8) Cut omelet into 3 even portions and serve.

Meal Prep Tip: In a resealable plastic bag, place the cooled omelet slices and seal the bag. Refrigerate for about 2-4 days. Reheat in the microwave on High for about 1 minute before serving.

Nutrition Information:

Calories per serving: 265; Carbohydrates: 1.5g; Protein: 14.7g; Fat: 22.4g; Sugar: 0g; Sodium: 241mg; Fiber: 0g

Lunch: Summary Lunch Soup

Serves: 6

Cooking Time: 35 minutes

Preparation Time: 15 minutes

Ingredients:

- 2 tablespoons unsalted butter
- 2 yellow onions, chopped
- 6 garlic cloves, minced
- 6 cups yellow squash, seeded and cubed
- 4 thyme sprigs
- 4 cups homemade vegetable broth
- Salt and freshly ground black pepper, to taste
- 2 tablespoons fresh lemon juice
- 4 tablespoons Parmesan cheese, shredded
- 2 teaspoons fresh lemon peel, grated finely

Instructions:

1) In a large pot, melt butter over medium heat and sauté onions for 5-6 minutes.
2) Add garlic and sauté for 1 minute.
3) Add squash and cook for 5 minutes.
4) Add thyme, broth, salt and black pepper. Bring to a boil.
5) Reduce the heat to low and simmer while covered for 15-20 minutes.
6) Turn fire off. Discard the thyme sprigs.
7) Set aside to cool slightly.
8) With a handheld blender, puree soup until smooth.
9) Return pot over medium heat.
10) Stir in lemon juice and cook for about 2-3 minutes or until heated completely.
11) Serve hot with the garnishing of cheese and lemon peel.

Meal Prep Tip: Once soup has cooled, evenly divide the mixture into 6 containers. Cover the containers and refrigerate for 1-2 days. Reheat in the microwave before serving.

Nutrition Information:

Calories per serving: 86; Carbohydrates: 9g; Protein: 3.7g; Fat: 4.4g; Sugar: 3.7g; Sodium: 129mg; Fiber: 2.2g

Dinner: Lovely Steak Dinner

Serves: 6

Cooking Time: 10 minutes

Preparation Time: 20 minutes

Ingredients:

- 1 (2-pound) grass-fed flat iron steak
- Salt and freshly ground black pepper, to taste
- 2 tablespoons olive oil
- 1 large yellow onion, sliced thinly
- ½ cup Italian dressing
- 2 Portobello mushrooms, sliced
- 3 large red bell peppers, seeded and sliced thinly
- 1/3 cup homemade chicken broth
- ½ cup blue cheese, crumbled

Instructions:

1) Preheat the grill to medium-high heat. Grease the grill grate.
2) Sprinkle the steak with salt and black pepper generously.
3) Grill the steak for about 5 minutes per side.
4) Transfer the steak onto a cutting board. Let it rest for about 10 minutes before slicing.
5) With a sharp knife, cut the beef steak diagonally across grain in desired size.
6) Meanwhile, in a skillet, heat oil on medium-high heat and sauté onion for about 4 minutes.
7) Add Italian dressing and bring to a boil.
8) Reduce the heat to medium.
9) Add mushrooms and bell pepper and cook for about 5 minutes, stirring occasionally.
10) With a slotted spoon, transfer the vegetables into a bowl.
11) Add the broth in skillet and immediately increase the heat to medium-high.
12) Cook for about 5 minutes or until desired thickness of sauce, stirring frequently.

13) Divide vegetable mixture onto serving plates and top with steak slices.

14) Sprinkle with cheese and serve.

Meal Prep Tip: Let Lovely Steak Dinner to cool completely. Evenly divide into 6 containers. Cover the containers and refrigerate for up to 3-4 days. Reheat in the microwave before serving.

Nutrition Information:

Calories per serving: 535; Carbohydrates: 10.3g; Protein: 51.9g; Fat: 31.4g; Sugar: 5.9g; Sodium: 358mg; Fiber: 1.8g

Day 4

Breakfast: Savory Cheese Waffles

Serves: 6

Cooking Time: 36 minutes

Preparation Time: 15 minutes

Ingredients:
- 1 cup cauliflower, processed into a coarse crumb
- 2 organic eggs, beaten
- 1 cup mozzarella cheese, shredded finely
- 1/3 cup Parmesan cheese, shredded finely
- 1 tablespoon chives, minced
- 1 teaspoon onion powder
- 1 teaspoon garlic powder
- ½ teaspoon freshly ground black pepper

Instructions:
1) Preheat the waffle iron and then lightly grease with cooking spray.
2) In a large bowl, add all ingredients and mix until well combined.
3) Place ¼ of the mixture into preheated waffle iron and cook for about 4-6 minutes or until golden brown.
4) Repeat with the remaining mixture.

Meal Prep Tip: Let waffles cool completely. Store each waffle in a zip lock bag and freeze. It will last as long as 2 to 4 weeks in the freezer. Reheat in the microwave before serving.

Nutrition Information:
Calories per serving: 97; Carbohydrates: 2.4g; Protein: 8.7g; Fat: 6g; Sugar: 0.8g; Sodium: 280mg; Fiber: 0.6g

Lunch: Nicely Braised Cabbage

Serves: 4

Cooking Time: 25 minutes

Preparation Time: 15 minutes

Ingredients:

- 1½ teaspoons butter
- 2½ cups green cabbage, chopped
- 1 garlic clove, chopped
- 1 yellow onion, sliced thinly
- 1 cup homemade vegetable broth
- Salt, to taste

Instructions:

1) In a large nonstick skillet, melt butter over high heat and sauté cabbage, garlic and onion for about 5 minutes.
2) Gradually, stir in broth and immediately, reduce the heat to low.
3) Stir in salt and cook while covered for about 20 minutes.
4) Serve warm.

Meal Prep Tip: Transfer the cabbage mixture into a large bowl and set aside to cool completely. Divide the mixture evenly into 4 containers. Cover the containers and refrigerate for about 2 days. Reheat in the microwave before serving. Sprinkle with cheese just before serving.

Nutrition Information:

Calories per serving: 45; Carbohydrates: 5.6g; Protein: 2.1g; Fat: 1.8g; Sugar: 2.8g; Sodium: 249mg; Fiber: 1.7g

Dinner: Corned Beef in Slow Cooker

Serves: 6

Cooking Time: 9 hours

Preparation Time: 10 minutes

Ingredients:

- 2 cups water
- 2-pounds corned beef brisket with seasoning packet
- 1 cabbage, cut into wedges
- 2 onions, chopped

Instructions:

1) In cold running water, rinse corned beef and then dry with paper towels.
2) Place corned beef in slow cooker and sprinkle seasoning packet.
3) Add onions, cabbage, and water.
4) Cover and cook on low for 9 hours.
5) Let it cool, evenly divide into suggested servings, and store in meal prep ready container.

Meal Prep Tip: Let corned beef cool completely. Evenly divide into 6 containers evenly. Cover the containers and refrigerate for up to 3-4 days. Reheat in the microwave before serving.

Nutrition Information:

Calories per serving: 314; Carbohydrates: 3.6g; Protein: 22.6g; Fat: 22.6g; Sugar: 3.9g; Sodium: 358mg; Fiber: 0.6g

Day 5

Breakfast: Crunchy Granola

Serves: 10

Cooking Time: 18 minutes

Preparation Time: 15 minutes

Ingredients:

- 1½ cups almonds
- 1½ cups hazelnuts
- ¼ cup cacao powder
- 1 cup flax seeds meal
- Pinch of sea salt
- ¼ cup hazelnut oil
- ¼ cup almond butter, melted
- 2-ounce unsweetened dark chocolate, chopped
- 1/3 cup erythritol
- 20 drops stevia extract

Instructions:

1) Preheat the oven to 300 degrees F. Line a large baking sheet with parchment paper.
2) In a food processor, add almonds and hazelnuts and pulse until a coarse crumb form.
3) Transfer the nut mixture into a large bowl.
4) Add cacao powder, flax seeds meal and salt. Mix well.
5) In a pan, add hazelnut oil, butter and chocolate over low heat and cook for about 2-3 minutes or until smooth, stirring continuously.
6) Stir in stevia and erythritol. Immediately remove from heat.
7) Add butter mixture over nut mixture and toss to coat well.
8) Transfer the mixture onto prepared baking sheet evenly.
9) Bake for about 15 minutes, stirring after every 5 minutes.

10) Turn off the oven but keep the baking sheet in oven for about 20 minutes, stirring occasionally.

11) Remove from oven and set aside to cool completely.

Meal Prep Tip: Transfer granola in an airtight container and store in a cool, dry place for up to 2 weeks.

Nutrition Information:

Calories per serving: 280; Carbohydrates: 12g; Protein: 9.2g; Fat: 23.1g; Sugar: 1.1g; Sodium: 26mg; Fiber: 7g

Lunch: Restaurant Style Crab Salad

Serves: 6

Preparation Time: 15 minutes

Ingredients:

- 1 pound jumbo lump crabmeat, picked over
- 1 celery stalk, peeled, and cut into 1/8-inch pieces
- 4 teaspoons fresh chives, minced
- 1 teaspoon fresh tarragon leaves, minced
- 1/3 cup mayonnaise
- tablespoons sour cream
- 1 teaspoon fresh lemon juice
- ½ teaspoon Dijon mustard
- Salt and freshly ground black pepper, to taste

Instructions:

1) In a bowl, add the crabmeat, celery, chives and tarragon and toss to coat well.
2) In another bowl, add the mayonnaise, sour cream, lemon juice, mustard, salt and pepper and mix until well combined.
3) Add the dressing to the crabmeat mixture and gently, stir to combine.
4) Serve immediately.

Meal Prep Tip: In 6 containers, divide salad and refrigerate for about 1 day.

Nutrition Information:

Calories per serving: 124; Carbohydrates: 4.8g; Protein: 9.7g; Fat: 6.2g; Sugar: 0.9g; Sodium: 600mg; Fiber: 0.1g

Dinner: Tummy Satisfying Soup

Serves: 4

Cooking Time: 30 minutes

Preparation Time: 15 minutes

Ingredients:

- 1 pound grass-fed ground beef
- ½ pound fresh mushrooms, sliced
- 1 small onion, chopped
- 1 garlic clove, minced
- 1 pound head bok choy, stalks and leaves separated and chopped
- 4 cups homemade chicken broth
- Salt and freshly ground black pepper, to taste

Instructions:

1) Heat a large nonstick soup pan over medium-high heat and cook beef for 5 minutes.
2) Add onion, mushrooms and garlic. Cook for 5 minutes.
3) Add bok choy stalks and cook for about 4-5 minutes.
4) Add broth and bring to a boil.
5) Reduce the heat to low and simmer, covered for about 10 minutes.
6) Stir in bok choy leaves and simmer for about 5 minutes.
7) Stir in salt and black pepper and remove from heat.
8) Serve hot.

Meal Prep Tip: Transfer the soup into a large bowl and set aside to cool. Divide the mixture into 4 containers evenly. Cover the containers and refrigerate for 1-2 days. Reheat in the microwave before serving.

Nutrition Information:

Calories per serving: 325; Carbohydrates: 7.9g; Protein: 43.6g; Fat: 12.9g; Sugar: 3.8g; Sodium: 926mg; Fiber: 2.1g

Day 6

Breakfast: Spanish Scramble

Serves: 2

Cooking Time: 8 minutes

Preparation Time: 15 minutes

Ingredients:

- 1/3 cup heavy cream
- 4 large organic eggs
- 2 tablespoons fresh cilantro, chopped finely
- Salt and freshly ground black pepper, to taste
- 3 tablespoons butter
- 1 small tomato, chopped
- 1 Serrano chili pepper
- 2 tablespoons scallions, sliced thinly

Instructions:

1) In a bowl, add the cream, eggs, cilantro, salt and pepper. Beat until well combined.
2) In a large nonstick frying pan, melt the butter over medium heat and sauté tomato and Serrano pepper for about 2 minutes.
1) Add the egg mixture and cook for 3-4 minutes, stirring continuously.
3) Garnish with the scallions and serve.

Meal Prep Tip: Transfer the cooled Spanish Scramble into airtight container and refrigerate for up to 3 days. Reheat in microwave before serving.

Nutrition Information:

Calories per serving: 378; Carbohydrates: 4.1g; Protein: 13.7g; Fat: 34.7g; Sugar: 2.2g; Sodium: 541mg; Fiber: 0.7g

Lunch: Fancy Luncheon Salad

Serves: 8

Preparation Time: 15 minutes

Ingredients:

- 12 hard-boiled eggs, peeled and cubed
- 8-ounce cooked salmon, chopped
- 2 celery stalks, chopped
- 1 yellow onion, chopped
- 3 tablespoons fresh dill, chopped
- 1½ cups mayonnaise
- Salt and freshly ground black pepper, to taste

Instructions:

1) In a large serving bowl, add all ingredients and gently stir to combine.
2) Cover and refrigerate to chill before serving.

Meal Prep Tip: In 8 containers, divide salad and refrigerate for about 1 day.

Nutrition Information:

Calories per serving: 313; Carbohydrates: 12g; Protein: 14.6g; Fat: 23.1g; Sugar: 4g; Sodium: 444mg; Fiber: 20.5g

Dinner: Indian Butter Chicken

Serves: 5

Cooking Time: 21 minutes

Preparation Time: 15 minutes

Ingredients:

- 2 tablespoons unsalted butter
- 1 medium onion, chopped
- 2 garlic cloves, minced
- 1 teaspoon fresh ginger, minced
- 1½ pounds grass-fed chicken breasts, cut into ¾-inch chunks
- 1 (6-ounce) can sugar-free tomato paste
- 1 tablespoon garam masala
- 1 teaspoon red chili powder
- 1 teaspoon fenugreek seeds
- 1 teaspoon ground cumin
- Salt and freshly ground black pepper, to taste
- 1 cup heavy cream

Instructions:

1) In a large skillet, melt butter over medium-high heat and sauté onions for 3-4 minutes.
2) Add garlic and ginger and sauté for 1 minute.
3) Add the chicken, tomato paste and spices and cook for about 6 minutes or until desired doneness of chicken is achieved.
4) Stir in the heavy cream and simmer for about 8-10 minutes, stirring occasionally.
5) Serve hot.

Meal Prep Tip: Transfer the chicken mixture into a large bowl and set aside to cool completely. Divide the mixture into 5 containers evenly. Cover the containers and refrigerate for up to 3-4 days. Reheat in the microwave before serving.

Nutrition Information:

Calories per serving: 427; Carbohydrates: 10.7g; Protein:.42.1g; Fat: 24g; Sugar: 5.2g; Sodium: 202mg; Fiber: 2.3g

Day 7

Breakfast: French Style Crepes

Serves: 2

Cooking Time: 12 minutes

Preparation Time: 15 minutes

Ingredients:

- 2 tablespoons coconut oil, melted and divided
- 2 organic eggs
- 1 teaspoon Splenda
- 1/8 teaspoon sea salt
- 2 tablespoons coconut flour
- 1/3 cup heavy cream

Instructions:

1) In a bowl, add 1 tablespoon of oil, eggs, Splenda and salt. Beat until well combined.
2) Slowly, add flour, beating continuously until well combined.
3) Add heavy cream and stir until well combined.
4) Grease a large non-stick skillet with remaining oil.
5) Add ¼ of the mixture and tilt the pan to spread into a thin layer.
6) Cook for about 3 minutes, flipping once after 2 minutes.
7) Repeat with the remaining mixture.

Meal Prep Tip: Keep the crepes aside to cool completely before storing. With a plastic wrap, cover the crepes and refrigerate up to 2 days. Reheat each crepe in the microwave for about 30 seconds.

Nutrition Information:

Calories per serving: 319; Carbohydrates: 10.9g; Protein: 8g; Fat: 27.4g; Sugar: 3.4g; Sodium: 246mg; Fiber: 5.7g

Lunch: Cranberry Gravy on Beef Brisket

Serves: 8

Cooking Time: 8 hours

Preparation Time: 15 minutes

Ingredients:

- 12 large carrots, peeled and cut into 2-inch long sticks
- ½ teaspoon salt
- ¼ teaspoon pepper
- ½ cup chopped onion
- 1 (8-ounce) can tomato sauce
- 1 (14-ounce) whole-berry cranberry sauce
- 1 fresh beef brisket (2 ½-pounds)
- 1 tablespoon prepared mustard

Instructions:

1) Chop beef into 1-inch cubes and spread on bottom of slow cooker.
2) Add remaining ingredients into pot.
3) Cover and cook on low for 8 hours.
4) Serve hot.

Meal Prep Tip: Let dish cool completely. Divide the mixture evenly into 7 containers. Cover the containers and refrigerate for about 3-4 days. Reheat in the microwave before serving. Sprinkle with the cheese just before serving.

Nutrition Information:

Calories per serving: 264; Carbohydrates: 29.7g; Protein: 24.9g; Fat: 24.4g; Sugar: 4.6g; Sodium: 84mg; Fiber: 2.7g

Dinner: Classic Steak Meal

Serves: 4

Cooking Time: 20 minutes

Preparation Time: 15 minutes

Ingredients for Steak Sauce:

- 2 tablespoons butter
- 2 tablespoons yellow onion
- 2 garlic cloves, minced
- 1 teaspoon fresh thyme, chopped finely
- 1 1/3 cups homemade beef broth
- 2 tablespoons fresh lemon juice
- ¾ cup fresh blueberries

Ingredients for Steak:

- 1 tablespoon butter
- 4 (6-ounce) grass-fed flank steaks
- Salt and freshly ground black pepper, to taste

Instructions:

1) For sauce: in a pan, melt butter over medium heat and sauté onion for about 2 minutes.
2) Add garlic and thyme and sauté for about 1 minute.
3) Add broth and broth and bring to a gentle simmer.
4) Reduce the heat to low and simmer for about 10 minutes.
5) Meanwhile, for steak in a skillet, melt butter over medium-high heat and cook steaks with salt and black pepper for about 3-4 minutes per side.
6) Transfer the steak into a bowl.
7) Add sauce in the skillet and stir to scrap up the brown bits.
8) Stir in lemon juice, blueberries, salt and black pepper and cook for about 1-2 minutes.
9) Serve the steaks with the topping of sauce.

Meal Prep Tip: Transfer the steak with into a large bowl and set aside to cool completely. Divide the mixture into 4 containers evenly. Cover the containers and refrigerate for up to 3-4 days. Reheat in the microwave before serving.

Nutrition Information:

Calories per serving: 445; Carbohydrates: 5.5g; Protein: 49.5g; Fat: 24g; Sugar: 3.3g; Sodium: 432mg; Fiber: 0.9g

Day 8

Breakfast: Satisfying Veggie Frittata

Serves: 5

Cooking Time: 25 minutes

Preparation Time: 15 minutes

Ingredients:

- 12 organic egg whites
- Salt and freshly ground black pepper, to taste
- 2 teaspoons olive oil
- 1 garlic clove, minced
- 3 cups fresh baby spinach, chopped
- 1 large zucchini, spiralized with Blade C
- 2-ounce feta cheese, crumbled

Instructions:

1) Preheat the oven to 375 degrees F.
2) In a large bowl, add egg whites, salt and pepper. Beat well.
3) In an oven proof skillet, heat oil over medium heat and sauté garlic for about 1 minute.
4) Add spinach and cook for about 2-3 minutes.
5) Transfer half of spinach into a bowl.
6) Place zucchini over spinach in the skillet evenly and top with the remaining spinach, followed by the egg white mixture.
7) Sprinkle with cheese evenly and slightly push into egg whites.
8) Bake for about 15-20 minutes or until top becomes golden brown.
9) Remove from oven and keep onto a wire rack for about 5 minutes before slicing.
10) Cut into 5 equal slices and serve.

Meal Prep Tip: In a resealable plastic bag, place the cooled frittata slices and seal the bag. Refrigerate for about 2-4 days. Reheat in the microwave on High for about 1 minute before serving.

Nutrition Information:

Calories per serving: 102; Carbohydrates: 4.1g; Protein: 19.4g; Fat: 4.6g; Sugar: 1.9g; Sodium: 258mg; Fiber: 1.4g

Lunch: Hearty Saucy Meatballs

Serves: 6

Cooking Time: 45 minutes

Preparation Time: 20 minutes

Ingredients for Meatballs:

- 1 pound grass-fed lean ground lamb
- 1 tablespoon sugar-free tomato paste
- ¼ cup fresh coriander leaves, chopped
- 1 small yellow onion, chopped finely
- 2 garlic cloves, minced
- ½ teaspoon ground cumin
- Freshly ground black pepper, to taste

Ingredients for Tomato Gravy:

- 3 tablespoons olive oil, divided
- 1 large yellow onions, chopped finely
- 2 garlic cloves, minced
- ½ tablespoon fresh ginger, minced
- 1 teaspoon dried thyme, crushed
- 1 teaspoon ground cumin
- 1 teaspoon cayenne pepper
- 3 large tomatoes, chopped finely
- Salt and freshly ground black pepper, to taste
- 1½ cups warm homemade chicken broth

Instructions:

1) For meatballs: in a large bowl, add all ingredients and mix until well combined.
2) Make small equal sized balls from mixture and set aside.
3) For gravy: in a large pan, heat 1 tablespoon of oil over medium heat.

4) Add meatballs and cook for about 4-5 minutes or until lightly browned from all sides.

5) Transfer the meatballs onto a plate.

6) In the same pan, heat remaining oil over medium heat.

7) Add onion and sauté for about 8-10 minutes.

8) Add garlic, ginger, thyme and spices and sauté for about 1 minute.

9) Add tomatoes and cook for about 3-4 minutes, crushing with the back of spoon.

10) Add warm broth and bring to a boil.

11) Carefully, place meatballs and cook for 5 minutes, without stirring.

12) Reduce the heat to low and coo, partially covered for about 15-20 minutes, stirring carefully 2-3 times.

13) Serve hot.

Meal Prep Tip: Transfer the meatballs mixture into a large bowl and set aside to cool completely. Divide the mixture into 6 containers evenly. Cover the containers and refrigerate for up to 3-4 days. Reheat in the microwave before serving.

Nutrition Information:

Calories per serving: 250; Carbohydrates: 9.1g; Protein: 24g; Fat: 13.3g; Sugar: 4.5g; Sodium: 285mg; Fiber: 2.3g

Dinner: Filling Chicken Soup

Serves: 6

Cooking Time: 35 minutes

Preparation Time: 15 minutes

Ingredients:

- 2 tablespoons butter
- ½ cup yellow onion, chopped
- 2 celery stalks, chopped
- 1 garlic clove, minced
- 2 teaspoons xanthan gum
- 1 teaspoon dried parsley, crushed
- 1 teaspoon freshly ground black pepper
- 4 cups homemade chicken broth
- 12-ounce cauliflower, chopped
- 2 cups cooked grass-fed chicken, chopped
- 2 cups heavy cream
- ¼ cup fresh parsley, chopped

Instructions:

1) In a large soup pan, melt butter over medium heat and sauté onion and celery for about 4-5 minutes.
2) Add garlic and sauté for about 1 minute.
3) Meanwhile, in a bowl, mix together xanthan gum, parsley and black pepper.
4) Sprinkle the soup with parsley mixture and stir to combine.
5) Add broth and cauliflower and bring to a boil.
6) Reduce the heat to low and simmer, covered for about 20 minutes, stirring occasionally.
7) Stir in cooked chicken, cream, parsley and salt and simmer for about 3-4 minutes.
8) Serve hot.

Meal Prep Tip: Transfer the soup into a large bowl and set aside to cool. Divide the mixture into 6 containers evenly. Cover the containers and refrigerate for 1-2 days. Reheat in the microwave before serving.

Nutrition Information:

Calories per serving: 280; Carbohydrates: 8g; Protein: 17.2g; Fat: 20.2g; Sugar: 2.4g; Sodium: 171mg; Fiber: 2.7g

Day 9

Breakfast: Convenient Breakfast Cereal

Serves: 16

Cooking Time: 25 minutes

Preparation Time: 10 minutes

Ingredients:

- 1 tablespoon ground cinnamon
- 1 teaspoon ground nutmeg
- 1 tablespoon plus 1 teaspoon organic vanilla extract
- ½ teaspoon stevia powder
- ½ cup water
- 1 pound unsweetened coconut flakes

Instructions:

1) Preheat the oven to 300 degrees F. Line 3 cookie sheets with parchment paper.
2) In a large bowl, add all ingredients except coconut flakes and beat until well combined.
3) Transfer the coconut flakes in prepared cookie sheets evenly.
4) Bake for about 15 minutes.
5) Remove the cookie sheets from oven and stir in the flakes.
6) Bake for 5-10 minutes more.
7) Remove from oven and set aside to cool completely.
8) You can enjoy this cereal with any non-dairy milk and keto-approved nuts.

Meal Prep Tip: Transfer this cereal into an airtight container and preserve in refrigerator for 2-4 weeks.

Nutrition Information:

Calories per serving: 136; Carbohydrates: 8.1g; Protein: 1.9g; Fat: 11.4g; Sugar: 0.2g; Sodium: 0mg; Fiber: 4g

Lunch: Best-Ever Tuna Salad

Serves: 2

Preparation Time: 15 minutes

Ingredients:

- 6 hard-boiled organic eggs, peeled and chopped
- 2/3 cup mayonnaise
- ½ teaspoon seasoned salt
- ½ cup cucumber, chopped
- 1 (5-ounce) can water packed tuna, drained
- 3 cups fresh baby arugula

Instructions:

1) In a large bowl, mix together egg, mayonnaise and seasoned salt.
2) Add remaining ingredients and gently stir to combine.
3) Serve chilled or at room temperature.

Meal Prep Tip: Divide egg mixture in 2 mason jars evenly. Place the remaining ingredients in the layers of cucumber, tuna and arugula. Cover each jar with the lid tightly and refrigerate for about 1 day. Shake the jars well just before serving.

Nutrition Information:

Calories per serving: 481; Carbohydrates: 8.6g; Protein: 24.9g; Fat: 39.2g; Sugar: 4.9g; Sodium: 600mg; Fiber: 0.4g

Dinner: Zoodles Lasagna

Serves: 4

Cooking Time: 45 minutes

Preparation Time: 20 minutes

Ingredients:

- 1 large zucchini
- Salt, to taste
- 1 pound grass-fed ground beef
- 1 cup sugar-free marinara sauce
- Freshly ground black pepper, to taste
- 10-ounce ricotta cheese
- 4-ounce mozzarella cheese, shredded

Instructions:

1) With a vegetable peeler, peel zucchini into strips, leaving the core.
2) Sprinkle the zucchini strips with salt and set aside in a colander for about 15 minutes.
3) Carefully, squeeze out the zucchini strips to remove moisture.
4) Preheat the oven to 350 degrees F.
5) Heat a nonstick skillet and cook the ground beef for about 8-10 minutes.
6) Stir in the marinara sauce, salt and pepper and remove from the heat.
7) In a casserole dish, place the beef evenly, followed by the zucchini, ricotta and mozzarella.
8) With a piece of foil, cover the casserole dish and bake for about 30 minutes.
9) Now, set the oven to broiler.
10) Remove the foil and broil for about 2-3 minutes.
11) Cut into desired sized pieces and serve.

Meal Prep Tip: Remove the casserole from oven and set aside to cool completely. In 4 containers, divide the casserole pieces evenly and refrigerate for about 2 days. Reheat in microwave before serving.

Nutrition Information:

Calories per serving: 291; Carbohydrates: 12.4g; Protein:.23.6g; Fat: 16.4g; Sugar: 4.6g; Sodium: 500mg; Fiber: 1.9g

Day 10

Breakfast: Healthy Spinach Quiche

Serves: 6

Cooking Time: 38 minutes

Preparation Time: 15 minutes

Ingredients:

- 1 tablespoon olive oil
- 1 onion, chopped
- 1 (10-ounce) package frozen spinach, thawed
- 3 cups Muenster cheese, shredded
- 5 organic eggs, beaten
- Salt and freshly ground black pepper, to taste

Instructions:

1) Preheat the oven to 350 degrees F. Lightly grease a 9-inch pie dish.
2) In a large skillet, heat oil over medium heat and sauté onion for about 4-5 minutes.
3) Increase the heat to medium-high.
4) Add spinach and cook for about 2-3 minutes or until all the liquid is absorbed.
5) Remove from heat and set aside to cool slightly.
6) Meanwhile in a large bowl, mix together remaining ingredients.
7) Add spinach mixture and stir to combine.
8) Transfer the mixture into prepared pie dish.
9) Bake for about 30 minutes.
10) Remove from the oven and set aside to cool for about 10 minutes before serving.
11) Cut into 6 equal sized wedges and serve.

Meal Prep Tip: In a reseal able plastic bag, place the cooled quiche slices and seal the bag. Refrigerate for about 2-4 days. Reheat in the microwave on High for about 1 minute before serving.

Nutrition Information:

Calories per serving: 299; Carbohydrates: .4g; Protein: 19.4g; Fat: 23.1g; Sugar: 1.9g; Sodium: 471mg; Fiber: 1.4g

Lunch: Baked Herbed Salmon

Serves: 4

Cooking Time: 15 minutes

Preparation Time: 15 minutes

Ingredients:

- 1 tablespoon butter
- ¼ tsp tarragon
- ¼ tsp thyme
- ½ cup soy sauce
- ½ tsp basil
- ½ tsp ground ginger
- ½ tsp rosemary
- 1 tsp minced garlic
- 1 tsp oregano leaves
- 2 pounds salmon fillet
- 1 tbsp sesame oil

Instructions:

1) In a Ziploc back, place the sesame oil, soy sauce and spices and shake thoroughly until well combined. Put the salmon pieces in the Ziploc bag. Refrigerate the salmon with the marinade for 4 hours.

2) Preheat the oven to 350oF. Place the marinated salmon on a baking pan lined with aluminum foil.

3) Bake the marinated salmon for 15 minutes.

4) Serve hot.

Meal Prep Tip: Let salmon cool. Evenly divide the mixture into 4 containers. Cover the containers and refrigerate for 3 days. Reheat in the microwave before serving. Sprinkle with the cheese just before serving.

Nutrition Information:

Calories per serving: 448; Carbohydrates: 8.6g; Protein: 50.7g; Fat: 21.9g; Sugar: 3.6g; Sodium: 70mg; Fiber: 0.9g

Dinner: Rich-Flavored Stew

Serves: 8

Cooking Time: 2 hours 10 minutes

Preparation Time: 15 minutes

Ingredients:

- 2 pounds grass-fed beef stew meat, trimmed and cubed into 1-inch size
- 1 1/3 cups homemade hot chicken broth
- 2 yellow onions, chopped
- 2 bay leaves
- 1 teaspoon Greek seasoning
- Freshly ground black pepper, to taste
- 3 celery stalks, chopped
- 1 (8-ounce) package shredded cabbage
- 1 (8-ounce) can sugar-free tomato sauce
- 1 (8-ounce) can sugar-free whole plum tomatoes, chopped roughly with liquid
- Salt, to taste

Instructions:

1) Heat a large nonstick pan over medium-high heat and cook beef for 5 minutes or until browned.
2) Drain excess grease from the pan.
3) Stir in the broth, onion, bay leaves, Greek seasoning and black pepper. Bring to a boil.
4) Reduce the heat to low and simmer while covered for about 1¼ hours.
5) Stir in celery and cabbage. Simmer while covered for about 30 minutes.
6) Stir in tomato sauce and chopped plum tomatoes and simmer uncovered for about 20 minutes.
7) Stir in salt and remove from heat.
8) Discard bay leaves and serve hot.

Meal Prep Tip: Transfer the stew into a large bowl and set aside to cool. Divide the mixture into 8 containers evenly. Cover the containers and refrigerate for 1-2 days. Reheat in the microwave before serving.

.

Nutrition Information:

Calories per serving: 254; Carbohydrates: 8.7g; Protein: 36.8g; Fat: 7.5g; Sugar: 5g; Sodium: 405mg; Fiber: 2.4g

Day 11

Breakfast: French Style Crepes

Serves: 2

Cooking Time: 12 minutes

Preparation Time: 15 minutes

Ingredients:

- 2 tablespoons coconut oil, melted and divided
- 2 organic eggs
- 1 teaspoon Splenda
- 1/8 teaspoon sea salt
- 2 tablespoons coconut flour
- 1/3 cup heavy cream

Instructions:

1) In a bowl, add 1 tablespoon of oil, eggs, Splenda and salt and beat until well combined.
2) Slowly, add flour, beating continuously until well combined.
3) Add heavy cream and stir until well combined.
4) Grease a large non-stick skillet with remaining oil.
5) Add ¼ of the mixture and tilt the pan to spread into a thin layer.
6) Cook for about 3 minutes, flipping once after 2 minutes.
7) Repeat with the remaining mixture.

Meal Prep Tip: Keep the crepes aside to cool completely before storing. With a plastic wrap, cover the crepes and refrigerate up to 2 days. Reheat each crepe in the microwave for about 30 seconds.

Nutrition Information:

Calories per serving: 319; Carbohydrates: 10.9g; Protein: 8g; Fat: 27.4g; Sugar: 3.4g; Sodium: 246mg; Fiber: 5.7g

Lunch: Yummy Salmon Burgers

Serves: 8

Cooking Time: 8 minutes

Preparation Time: 15 minutes

Ingredients:

- 1 organic egg
- 3 tablespoons sugar-free ranch dressing
- 1 (14-ounce) can pink salmon, drained and bones removed
- 2-ounce smoked salmon, chopped roughly
- 1/3 cup almond flour
- 2 tablespoons fresh parsley, chopped
- 1 teaspoon Cajun seasoning
- 2 tablespoons avocado oil

Instructions:

1) In a large bowl, add the egg and ranch dressing and beat until well combined.
2) Add remaining ingredients and gently, mix until well combined.
3) Make 8 equal sized patties from the mixture.
4) In a nonstick skillet, heat oil over medium heat and cook the patties in 2 batches for about 2 minutes per side.
5) Serve hot.

Meal Prep Tip: Remove the patties from heat and set aside to cool completely. Store in an airtight container, by placing parchment papers between the burgers to avoid the sticking. These burgers can be stored in the freezer for up to 3 weeks. Before serving, thaw the burgers and then reheat in microwave.

Nutrition Information:

Calories per serving: 140; Carbohydrates: 2.6g; Protein: 12.9g; Fat: 8.4g; Sugar: 0.4g; Sodium: 473mg; Fiber: 0.7g

Dinner: Holiday Dinner Casserole

Serves: 8

Cooking Time: 1¼ hours

Preparation Time: 15 minutes

Ingredients:

- 6 bacon slices, chopped
- 2 pounds grass-fed ground beef
- ½ cup yellow onion, chopped
- Salt and freshly ground black pepper, to taste
- 8-ounce cheddar cheese, shredded and divided
- 1 organic egg, beaten
- 16-ounce frozen green beans
- 3 tablespoons butter, divided
- 16-ounces frozen cauliflower
- ¼ cup sour cream

Instructions:

1) Preheat the oven to 350 degrees F. Lightly, grease a baking dish
2) Heat a large nonstick skillet over medium-high heat and cook bacon for about 8-10 minutes or until crisp.
3) Drain the excess fats and transfer the bacon into a bowl.
4) In the same skillet, add beef and cook for about 4-5 minutes.
5) Add onion and cook for about 4-5 minutes.
6) Drain the excess grease from skillet.
7) Stir in salt and black pepper and remove from heat.
8) Stir in ½ of cheese, egg and cooked bacon and transfer into a baking dish.
9) Meanwhile, in a pan of boiling water, add green beans and cook for about 4-5 minutes.
10) Drain well and transfer into a bowl.
11) Add 1 tablespoon of butter and some salt and mix.

12) In the same pan, add cauliflower and boil for about 10-12 minutes. Drain well.

13) In a food processor, add cauliflower, sour cream, remaining butter, a pinch of salt and black pepper and pulse until smooth.

14) Place green beans over beef mixture evenly and top with cauliflower mixture evenly, followed by the remaining cheese evenly.

15) Bake for about 35 minutes or until bubbly.

Meal Prep Tip: Remove the casserole from oven and set aside to cool completely. In 8 containers, divide the casserole pieces evenly and refrigerate for about 2 days. Reheat in microwave before serving.

Nutrition Information:

Calories per serving: 500; Carbohydrates: 8.7g; Protein:.50g; Fat: 29.1g; Sugar: 2.7g; Sodium: 668mg; Fiber: 3.5g

Day 12

Breakfast: 2-Minute Bread

Serves: 1

Cooking Time: 1¼ minutes

Preparation Time: 15 minutes

Ingredients:

- 1 teaspoon butter, melted
- 1 large organic egg
- 1 package Splenda
- 2 tablespoons flax seeds meal
- ½ teaspoon baking powder
- ¼ cup cheddar cheese, shredded

Instructions:

1) Coat a microwave safe mug with 1 teaspoon melted butter.
2) In a bowl, add remaining ingredients and mix well.
3) Transfer the mixture into prepared mug evenly and microwave on High for about 1 minute.
4) Flip the side of bread and microwave for about 10-15 seconds more.

Meal Prep Tip: In a reseal able plastic bag, place the bread and seal the bag after squeezing the excess air. Keep the bread away from direct sunlight and preserve in a cool and dry place for about 1-2 days.

Nutrition Information:

Calories per serving: 291; Carbohydrates: 7.7g; Protein: 16.4g; Fat: 23.2g; Sugar: 0.5g; Sodium: 280mg; Fiber: 4.1g

Lunch: Bright Colored Platter

Serves: 8

Cooking Time: 40 minutes

Preparation Time: 15 minutes

Ingredients:

- ¼ teaspoon fresh lemon peel, grated finely
- 2 teaspoons butter, melted
- Salt and freshly ground white pepper, to taste
- 4 cups grape tomatoes
- 1½ pounds fresh green beans, trimmed
- ½ cup Parmesan cheese, grated

Instructions:

1) Preheat the oven to 350 degrees F.
2) In a large bowl, mix together lemon peel, butter, salt and white pepper.
3) Add grape tomatoes and toss to coat well.
4) Transfer the tomato mixture into a roasting pan.
5) Roast for about 35-40 minutes, stirring once midway through cooking.
6) Meanwhile, in a pan of boiling water, arrange a steamer basket.
7) Place green beans in steamer basket and steam, covered for about 7-8 minutes.
8) Drain the green beans well.
9) Divide the green beans and tomatoes in serving plates.
10) Sprinkle with cheese and serve.

Meal Prep Tip: Transfer the green beans and tomatoes into a large bowl and set aside to cool completely. Divide the mixture into 8 containers evenly. Cover the containers and refrigerate for about 1-2 days. Reheat in the microwave before serving. Sprinkle with the cheese just before serving.

Nutrition Information:

Calories per serving: 110; Carbohydrates: 9.9g; Protein: 6.2g; Fat: 5.9g; Sugar: 3.6g; Sodium: 219mg; Fiber: 4g

Dinner: Enticing Chicken Meal

Serves: 4

Cooking Time: 20 minutes

Preparation Time: 15 minutes

Ingredients:

- 2 (6-ounce) grass-fed skinless, boneless chicken breasts, cut into ½-inch pieces
- 1 medium zucchini, chopped
- 1 cup fresh broccoli florets
- 1 small yellow onion, chopped
- 2 garlic cloves, minced
- 1 teaspoon Italian seasoning
- ½ teaspoon paprika
- Salt and freshly ground black pepper, to taste
- 2 tablespoons olive oil

Instructions:

1) Preheat the oven to 450 degrees F. Line a large baking dish with a piece of foil.
2) In a large bowl, add all ingredients and toss to coat well.
3) Transfer the chicken mixture into prepared baking dish in a single layer.
4) Bake for about 15-20 minutes or until the chicken is tender.
5) Remove from oven and serve hot.

Meal Prep Tip: Divide the cooled chicken mixture into 4 containers. Cover and store in refrigerator for up to 5 days. Reheat before serving.

Nutrition Information:

Calories per serving: 195; Carbohydrates: 5.6g; Protein: 20.5g; Fat: 10.6g; Sugar: 2.1g; Sodium: 83mg; Fiber: 1.6g

Day 13

Breakfast: Enjoyable Quiche

Serves: 12

Cooking Time: 30 minutes

Preparation Time: 15 minutes

Ingredients:

- 2 tablespoons olive oil
- 1 medium yellow onion, chopped finely
- 6-8-ounce cooked sausage, crumbled
- 2 cups heavy cream
- 12 large organic eggs
- ½ teaspoon red pepper flakes, crushed
- Salt and freshly ground black pepper, to taste
- 5 cups cheddar cheese, shredded

Instructions:

1) Preheat the oven to 350 degrees F. Grease 2 (10-inch) quiche pans.
2) In a skillet, heat oil over medium-low heat and sauté onion for about 4-5 minutes.
3) Transfer onion into a bowl and set aside to cool.
4) Add sausage and stir to combine.
5) In another bowl, add cream, eggs, red pepper flakes, salt and black pepper and beat until well combined.
6) Place cheese in the bottom of each prepared pan evenly, followed by sausage mixture and egg mixture.
7) With a fork, gently stir to combine.
8) Bake for about 20-25 minutes.
9) Remove from oven and keep onto a wire rack for about 5-10 minutes before slicing.
10) Cut into desired sized wedges and serve.

Meal Prep Tip: In a reseal able plastic bag, place the cooled quiche slices and seal the bag. Refrigerate for about 2-4 days. Reheat in the microwave on High for about 1 minute before serving.

Nutrition Information:

Calories per serving: 418; Carbohydrates: 2.5g; Protein: 22.2g; Fat: 35.7g; Sugar: 1.1g; Sodium: 524mg; Fiber: 0.2g

Lunch: Refreshingly Tangy Salad

Serves: 6

Preparation Time: 15 minutes

Ingredients for Salad:

- 4 cups green cabbage, shredded
- ¼ onion, sliced thinly
- 1 teaspoon lime zest, grated freshly
- 3 tablespoons fresh cilantro, chopped

Ingredients for Dressing:

- ¾ cup mayonnaise
- 2 teaspoons fresh lime juice
- 2 teaspoons chili sauce
- ½ teaspoon erythritol
- 2 garlic cloves, minced

Instructions:

1) In a large bowl, add all salad ingredients and toss to mix.
2) In another bowl, add all dressing ingredients and beat until well combined.
3) Pour dressing over salad and gently, toss to coat well.
4) Cover and refrigerate to chill before serving.

Meal Prep Tip: In 6 containers, divide salad and dressing equally. Refrigerate for about 2-3 days. Only when ready to eat do you add the dressing.

Nutrition Information:

Calories per serving: 130; Carbohydrates: 11g; Protein: 1g; Fat: 9.9g; Sugar: 4g; Sodium: 260mg; Fiber: 1.3g

Dinner: Indulgent Turkey Casserole

Serves: 9

Cooking Time: 1 hour

Preparation Time: 15 minutes

Ingredients:

- 2 medium zucchinis, sliced
- 2 medium tomatoes, sliced
- ¾ pound ground turkey
- 1 large yellow onion, chopped
- 2 garlic cloves, minced
- 1 cup sugar-free tomato sauce
- ½ cup cheddar cheese, shredded
- 2 cups cottage cheese, shredded
- 1 organic egg yolk
- 1 tablespoon fresh rosemary, minced
- Salt and freshly ground black pepper, to taste

Instructions:

1) Preheat the oven to 500 degrees F. Grease a large roasting pan.
2) Arrange zucchini and tomato slices into prepared roasting pan and spray with some cooking spray.
3) Roast for about 10-12 minutes.
4) Remove from oven.
5) Meanwhile, heat a non-stick skillet over medium-high heat and cook turkey for about 4-5 minutes or until browned.
6) Add onion and garlic and cook for about 4-5 minutes.
7) Stir in tomato sauce and cook for about 2-3 minutes.
8) Now, reduce the temperature of oven to 350 degrees F.
9) In a bowl, mix together remaining ingredients.

10) Transfer the turkey mixture into a 13x9-inch shallow baking dish and top with the roasted vegetables evenly.

11) Spread cheese mixture over vegetables evenly.

12) Bake for about 35 minutes.

13) Cut into equal sized 9 slices and serve.

Meal Prep Tip: Remove the turkey casserole from oven and set aside to cool completely. In 9 containers, divide the casserole slices evenly and refrigerate for about 2 days. Reheat in microwave before serving.

Nutrition Information:

Calories per serving: 209; Carbohydrates: 9g; Protein:.23g; Fat: 9g; Sugar: 4g; Sodium: 507mg; Fiber: 2g

Day 14

Breakfast: Fluffy Waffles

Serves: 10

Cooking Time: 50 minutes

Preparation Time: 15 minutes

Ingredients:

- 1 1/3 cups almond flour
- 2 tablespoons unsweetened vanilla whey protein powder
- 2 tablespoons Erythritol
- ½ teaspoon baking soda
- 1 teaspoon organic baking powder
- ½ teaspoon xanthan gum
- Salt, to taste
- 2 large organic eggs (whites and yolks separated)
- 2 organic whole eggs
- ¼ cup unsweetened almond milk
- 3 tablespoons butter
- 6-ounce fat-free Greek yogurt

Instructions:

1) Preheat the waffle iron and then grease it.
2) In a large bowl, add flour, protein powder, Erythritol, baking soda, baking powder, xanthan gum and salt and mix well.
3) In another small bowl, add egg whites and beat until stiff peaks form.
4) In a third bowl, add 2 egg yolks, whole eggs, almond milk, butter and yogurt and beat until well combined.
5) Add egg mixture into flour mixture and mix until well combined.
6) Gently, fold in beaten egg whites

7) Place ¼ cup of the mixture into preheated waffle iron and cook for about 4-5 minutes or until golden brown.

8) Repeat with the remaining mixture.

Meal Prep Tip: Store these waffles in a container by placing a piece of wax paper between each waffle. Refrigerate up to 2-3 days. Reheat in the microwave for about 1-2 minutes.

Nutrition Information:

Calories per serving: 102; Carbohydrates: 5.4g; Protein: 4.9g; Fat: 8.5g; Sugar: 4.4g; Sodium: 161mg; Fiber: 0.5g

Lunch: Ultimate Beef Burgers

Serves: 8

Cooking Time: 20 minutes

Preparation Time: 15 minutes

Ingredients:

- 1 pound grass-fed 80% ground beef
- 1 pound grass-fed ground brisket
- 2 tablespoons mayonnaise
- 1 tablespoon garlic, minced
- Salt and freshly ground black pepper, to taste
- ¼ cup butter, cut into 8 slices
- 2 tablespoons olive oil

Instructions:

1) In a bowl, add ground meat, mayonnaise, garlic, salt and black pepper and mix until well combined.

2) Make 8 equal sized patties from the mixture.

3) Place 1 butter slice inside each patty and cover with the meat.

4) In a large cast iron pan, heat oil over medium-low heat and cook burgers for about 10 minutes per side or until desired doneness, pressing with the spatula frequently.

5) Serve hot.

Meal Prep Tip: Remove the patties from heat and set aside to cool completely. Store in an airtight container, by placing parchment papers between the burgers to avoid the sticking. These burgers can be stored in refrigerator for about 1 day. Before serving, reheat in microwave.

Nutrition Information:

Calories per serving: 307; Carbohydrates: 1.2g; Protein: 34.6g; Fat: 17.6g; Sugar: 0.3g; Sodium: 142mg; Fiber: 0g

Dinner: Luscious Salmon

Serves: 8

Cooking Time: 23 minutes

Preparation Time: 15 minutes

Ingredients:

- 1/3 cup mayonnaise
- 2 garlic cloves, minced
- 2 tablespoons fresh lemon juice
- 1 tablespoon Dijon mustard
- 2 pounds salmon fillets
- 1 large yellow onion, sliced thinly
- Salt and freshly ground black pepper, to taste
- ¼ cup Parmesan cheese, shredded finely
- ½ cup Mozzarella cheese, shredded finely

Instructions:

1) Preheat the oven to 400 degrees F. Line a rimmed baking sheet with a piece of foil.
2) In a small bowl, add the mayonnaise, lemon juice, mustard and garlic and mix well.
3) Arrange the salmon fillet onto the prepared baking sheet and sprinkle with salt and pepper.
4) Place the onion slices over the salmon fillets evenly, followed by the mayonnaise mixture and cheeses.
5) Bake for about 15-18 minutes.
6) Now, set the oven to broiler.
7) Broil the salmon fillets for about 2-5 minutes.

Meal Prep Tip: Transfer the salmon mixture into a large bowl and set aside to cool completely. Divide the mixture into 8 containers evenly. Cover the containers and refrigerate for about 1 day. Reheat in the microwave before serving.

Nutrition Information:

Calories per serving: 327; Carbohydrates: 9.6g; Protein: 35.7g; Fat: 17.9g; Sugar: 2g; Sodium: 459mg; Fiber: 0.7g

Day 15

Breakfast: Holiday Morning Hash

Serves: 4

Cooking Time: 20 minutes

Preparation Time: 15 minutes

Ingredients:

- 3 cups cauliflower florets
- 2 tablespoons unsalted butter
- 1 small yellow onion, chopped
- 1 teaspoon dried thyme, crushed
- Salt and freshly ground black pepper, to taste
- 1 pound cooked turkey meat, chopped
- ¼ cup heavy cream

Instructions:

1) In a pan of salted boiling water, add cauliflower and cook for about 4 minutes.
2) Drain well and rinse under cold running water. Then chop the cauliflower and set aside.
3) In a large skillet, melt butter over medium heat and sauté onion for about 4-5 minutes.
4) Add thyme, salt and black pepper and sauté for about 1 minute.
5) Stir in cauliflower and cook for about 2 minutes.
6) Stir in turkey and cook for about 5-6 minutes.
7) Stir in cream and cook for about 2 minutes more.
8) Serve warm.

Meal Prep Tip: Transfer the cooled scramble into airtight container and refrigerate for up to 3 days. Reheat in microwave before serving.

Nutrition Information:

Calories per serving: 221; Carbohydrates: 21.3g; Protein: 18.6g; Fat: 10.5g; Sugar: 6g; Sodium: 600mg; Fiber: 2.9g

Lunch: Italian Tomato Salad

Serves: 2

Preparation Time: 15 minutes

Ingredients:

- ¼ cup fresh basil, chopped
- 1 garlic clove, minced
- 2 tablespoons extra-virgin olive oil
- 1 tablespoon balsamic vinegar
- Salt and freshly ground black pepper, to taste
- 2 medium ripe tomatoes, cut into slices
- 3-ounce mozzarella cheese, cubed
- 3 cups fresh arugula

Instructions:

1) In a small blender, add basil, garlic, olive oil, vinegar a pinch of salt and black pepper and pulse until smooth.
2) In a large serving bowl, mix together remaining ingredients.
3) Pour dressing and toss to coat well.
4) Serve immediately.

Meal Prep Tip: In 2 containers, divide salad and refrigerate for about 1 day.

Nutrition Information:

Calories per serving: 274; Carbohydrates: 8.1g; Protein: 14.1g; Fat: 22g; Sugar: 3.9g; Sodium: 347mg; Fiber: 2.1g

Dinner: Chicken Adobo

Serves: 4

Cooking Time: 35 minutes

Preparation Time: 15 minutes

Ingredients:

- ¼ cup vinegar
- ¼ cup water
- ½ cup coconut aminos
- 1 bay leaf
- 1 medium onion, chopped
- 1 tablespoon coconut oil
- 1 tablespoon whole peppercorns
- 4 garlic cloves, smashed and chopped roughly with skin
- 4-pieces chicken legs, skinless and cut into thigh and drumstick pieces

Instructions:

1) In a medium pot, add oil, and heat over medium high fire.
2) Once hot, sauté garlic for 2 minutes or until browned.
3) Add onions and sauté until soft and translucent, around 5 minutes.
4) Add chicken and peppercorn. Brown for 3 minutes per side.
5) Add soy sauce, peppercorns, vinegar, bay leaf, and water.
6) Bring to a simmer, lower fire to medium, and cover.
7) Cook for 15 minutes. Uncover and increase fire to medium high.
8) Continue cooking for 5 minutes or until more than half of the sauce has evaporated.
9) Serve.

Meal Prep Tip: Let it cool, evenly divide into suggested servings, and store in meal prep ready container. Refrigerate for 5-6 days. Reheat in the microwave before serving.

Nutrition Information:

Calories per serving: 293; Carbohydrates: 7.0g; Protein: 35.7g; Fat: 13.2g; Sugar: 5.7g; Sodium: 940mg; Fiber: 1.3g

Day 16

Breakfast: Richly Cheesy Muffins

Serves: 6

Cooking Time: 30 minutes

Preparation Time: 15 minutes

Ingredients:

- ½ cup almond meal
- ½ cup raw hemp seeds
- ¼ cup flax seeds meal
- ½ teaspoon baking powder
- ¼ cup nutritional yeast flakes
- Salt to taste
- ½ cup Parmesan cheese, grated finely
- ½ cup low-fat cottage cheese
- 6 organic eggs, beaten
- 1/3 cup scallion, sliced thinly

Instructions:

1) Preheat the oven to 375 degrees F. Grease 12 cups of a small muffin tin.
2) In a large bowl, add almond meal, hemp seeds, flax seeds meal, baking powder and salt and mix well.
3) In another bowl, add cottage cheese and eggs and mix well.
4) Add egg mixture into almond meal mixture and mix until well combined. Gently, fold in scallion.
5) Transfer the mixture into prepared muffin cups evenly.
6) Bake for about 25-30 minutes or until top becomes golden brown.
7) Serve warm.

Meal Prep Tip: Carefully invert the muffins onto a wire rack to cool completely. Line 1-2 airtight containers with paper towels. Arrange muffins over paper towel in a single layer. Cover muffins with another paper towel. Refrigerate for about 2-3 days. Reheat in the microwave on High for about 2 minutes before serving.

Nutrition Information:

Calories per serving: 306; Carbohydrates: 10.7g; Protein: 40.6g; Fat: 19.7g; Sugar: 1.3g; Sodium: 398mg; Fiber: 4.2g

Lunch: Super Quick Lunch

Serves: 4

Cooking Time: 6 minutes

Preparation Time: 15 minutes

Ingredients:

- 2 tablespoons olive oil
- 2 tablespoons unsalted butter
- 1 pound medium shrimp, peeled and deveined
- 1 small yellow onion, minced
- 4 garlic cloves, minced
- ¼ teaspoon red pepper flakes, crushed
- Salt and freshly ground black pepper, to taste
- ¼ cup homemade chicken broth
- 2 tablespoons fresh lemon juice
- 1 teaspoon fresh lemon zest, grated finely
- ½ pound zucchini, spiralized with Blade C
- 2 tablespoons Parmesan cheese, grated

Instructions:

1) In a large skillet, heat oil and butter over medium-high heat and cook shrimp, onion, garlic, red pepper flakes; salt and black pepper for about 2 minutes, stirring occasionally.
2) Stir in broth, lemon juice and lemon zest and bring to a gentle boil.
3) Stir in zucchini noodles and cook for about 1-2 minutes.
4) Serve hot.

Meal Prep Tip: Transfer the shrimp mixture into a large bowl and set aside to cool completely. Divide the mixture into 4 containers evenly. Cover the containers and refrigerate for about 1-2 days. Reheat in the microwave before serving.

Nutrition Information:

Calories per serving: 249; Carbohydrates: 4.9g; Protein: 26.3g; Fat: 14.7g; Sugar: 2g; Sodium: 459mg; Fiber: 1.2g

Dinner: Super-Healthy Chicken

Serves: 4

Cooking Time: 13 minutes

Preparation Time: 15 minutes

Ingredients:

- 2 tablespoons butter, divided
- 1 pound grass-fed chicken tenders
- Salt and freshly ground black pepper, to taste
- 2 garlic cloves, minced
- 10-ounces frozen chopped spinach, thawed
- ¼ cup Parmesan cheese, shredded
- ¼ cup heavy cream

Instructions:

1) In a large skillet, melt 1 tablespoon of butter over medium-high heat and cook the chicken with salt and black pepper for about 2 minutes from both sides.
2) Transfer the chicken into a bowl.
3) In the same skillet, melt remaining butter over medium-low heat and sauté garlic for about 1 minute.
4) Add spinach and cook for about 1 minute.
5) Add cheese, cream, salt and black pepper and stir to combine.
6) Spread the spinach mixture in the bottom of skillet evenly.
7) Place chicken over spinach in a single layer.
8) Immediately, reduce the heat to low and simmer, covered for about 5 minutes or until desired doneness of chicken.
9) Serve hot.

Meal Prep Tip: Transfer the chicken mixture into a large bowl and set aside to cool completely. Divide the mixture into 4 containers evenly. Cover the containers and refrigerate for up to 2 days. Reheat in the microwave before serving.

Nutrition Information:

Calories per serving: 394; Carbohydrates: 4g; Protein:.42.7g; Fat: 22.7g; Sugar: 0.3g; Sodium: 575mg; Fiber: 1.6g

Day 17

Breakfast: Incredibly Tasty Scramble

Serves: 6

Cooking Time: 10 minutes

Preparation Time: 15 minutes

Ingredients:

- 2 tablespoons unsalted butter
- 1 jalapeño pepper, chopped
- 1 small red onion, chopped
- 12 large organic eggs, beaten lightly
- Salt and freshly ground black pepper, to taste
- 2 tablespoons chives, chopped finely
- 4-ounce goat cheese, crumbled

Instructions:

1) In a large skillet, melt butter over medium heat and sauté jalapeño pepper and onion for about 4-5 minutes.
2) Add eggs, salt and black pepper and cook for about 3 minutes, stirring continuously.
3) Remove from heat and immediately, stir in chives and cheese.
4) Serve immediately.

Meal Prep Tip: Transfer the cooled scramble into airtight container and refrigerate for up to 3 days. Reheat in microwave before serving.

Nutrition Information:

Calories per serving: 268; Carbohydrates: 2.5g; Protein: 18.6g; Fat: 20.5g; Sugar: 1.8g; Sodium: 260mg; Fiber: 0.4g

Lunch: Jalapeño Poppers Soup

Serves: 5

Cooking Time: 35 minutes

Preparation Time: 15 minutes

Ingredients:

- 8 bacon slices, chopped
- 4 medium jalapeño peppers, seeded and chopped
- ¼ cup unsalted butter
- 1 teaspoon dried thyme, crushed
- ½ teaspoon ground cumin
- 3 cups homemade chicken broth
- 8-ounce cheddar cheese, shredded
- ¾ cup heavy cream
- Freshly ground black pepper, to taste

Instructions:

1) Heat a non-stick skillet over medium heat and cook bacon for about 8-10 minutes or until crisp.
2) Transfer the bacon onto a paper towel lined plate, reserving the grease in the skillet.
3) In the same skillet, add jalapeño peppers and sauté for about 1-2 minutes.
4) Transfer the jalapeño peppers into the plate with bacon
5) Transfer the remaining bacon grease in a large soup pan.
6) Add butter and heat over medium heat.
7) Add spices and sauté for about 1 minute.
8) Add broth and bring to a boil.
9) Reduce the heat to low and simmer for about 15 minutes.
10) Remove from heat and with an immersion blender, blend until smoot.
11) Return the pan over medium-low heat.

12) Stir in ¾ of the cooked bacon, cooked jalapeño, cheese, cream and black pepper and simmer for about 5 minutes.

13) Serve hot with the topping of remaining bacon.

Meal Prep Tip: Transfer the soup into a large bowl and set aside to cool. Divide the mixture into 5containers evenly. Cover the containers and refrigerate for 1-2 days. Reheat in the microwave before serving.

Nutrition Information:

Calories per serving: 592; Carbohydrates: 3.4g; Protein: 30.4g; Fat: 50.5g; Sugar: 0.7g; Sodium: 1500mg; Fiber: 0.6g

Dinner: Richly Creamy Steak

Serves: 4

Cooking Time: 1 hour

Preparation Time: 15 minutes

Ingredients:

- 4 cups heavy cream
- 3 tablespoons Parmesan cheese, shredded
- 3-ounce gorgonzola cheese, crumbled
- 1/8 teaspoon ground nutmeg
- Salt and freshly ground black pepper, to taste
- Pinch of onion powder
- Pinch of garlic powder
- Pinch of lemon pepper
- 4 (8-ounce) beef tenderloin steaks

Instructions:

1) In a pan, add heavy cream over medium heat and bring to a boil.
2) Reduce the heat to low and simmer for about 1 hour, stirring occasionally.
3) Remove from heat and immediately, stir in the both cheeses, nutmeg, salt and black prepper until well combined.
4) Meanwhile, in a small bowl, mix together onion powder, garlic powder, lemon pepper, salt and black pepper.
5) Sprinkle the steaks with seasoning mixture evenly.
6) Preheat the outdoor grill to medium-high heat. Grease the grill grate.
7) Grill the steaks for about 4-5 minutes from both sides or until desired doneness.
8) Place the steaks onto serving plates and top with the creamy sauce evenly.
9) Serve hot.

Meal Prep Tip: Transfer the steak with sauce into a large bowl and set aside to cool completely. Divide the mixture into 4 containers evenly. Cover the containers and refrigerate for up to 3-4 days. Reheat in the microwave before serving.

Nutrition Information:

Calories per serving: 915; Carbohydrates: 4.9g; Protein: 76.4g; Fat: 64.9g; Sugar: 0.2g; Sodium: 521mg; Fiber: 0.7g

Day 18

Breakfast: Perfect Breakfast Omelet

Serves: 2

Cooking Time: 15 minutes

Preparation Time: 15 minutes

Ingredients:

- 4 large organic eggs
- 1 tablespoon fresh chives, minced
- Salt and freshly ground black pepper, to taste
- 4 bacon slices
- 1 tablespoon unsalted butter
- 2-ounce cheddar cheese, shredded

Instructions:

1) In a bowl, add eggs, chives, salt and black pepper and beat until well combined.
2) Heat a non-stick frying pan over medium-high heat and cook bacon slices for about 8-10 minutes.
3) Transfer the bacon onto a paper towel lined plate to drain. Then chop the bacon slices.
4) With a paper towel, wipe out the frying pan.
5) In the same frying pan, melt the butter over medium-low heat and cook egg mixture for about 2 minutes.
6) Carefully, flip omelet and top with chopped bacon.
7) Cook for about 1-2 minutes or until desired doneness of eggs.
8) Remove from heat and immediately, place the cheese in the center of omelet.
9) Fold the edges of omelet over cheese and cut into 2 portions.
10) Serve immediately.

Meal Prep Tip: In a resealable plastic bag, place the cooled omelet slices and seal the bag. Refrigerate for about 2-4 days. Reheat in the microwave on High for about 1 minute before serving.

Nutrition Information:

Calories per serving: 622; Carbohydrates: 2g; Protein: 41.2g; Fat: 49.3g; Sugar: 1g; Sodium: 1500mg; Fiber: 0g

Lunch: Gourmet Sausage Platter

Serves: 4

Cooking Time: 15 minutes

Preparation Time: 15 minutes

Ingredients:

- 1 tablespoon olive oil
- 6 gluten-free Italian chicken sausages, sliced
- 1 large red bell pepper, seeded and sliced thinly
- 1 large green bell pepper, seeded and sliced thinly
- 1 large orange bell pepper, seeded and sliced thinly
- 1 teaspoon garlic powder
- Salt and freshly ground black pepper, to taste

Instructions:

1) In a large skillet, heat oil over medium-high heat and cook sausage for about 8-10 minutes.
2) Transfer the sausage slices into a large bowl and set aside.
3) In the same skillet, add bell peppers and garlic powder. Sauté for about 3-5 minutes.
4) Stir in sausage, salt and black pepper and remove from heat.
5) Serve hot.

Meal Prep Tip: Remove the sausage from heat and set aside to cool completely. In 4 containers, divide sausage mixture evenly and refrigerate for about 1 day. Reheat in microwave before serving.

Nutrition Information:

Calories per serving: 174; Carbohydrates: 11g; Protein:.25.9g; Fat:10.3; Sugar: 7g; Sodium: 281mg; Fiber: 4g

Dinner: Christmas Special Leg of Lamb

Serves: 12

Cooking Time: 1 hour 55 minutes

Preparation Time: 15 minutes

Ingredients:

- 1/3 cup fresh parsley, minced finely
- 8 garlic cloves, minced and divided
- 3 tablespoons olive oil, divided
- Salt and freshly ground black pepper, to taste
- 1 (4-pound) boneless leg of lamb, butterflied and trimmed
- 1/3 cup yellow onion, minced
- 4 cups fresh kale, trimmed and chopped
- ½ cup Kalamata olives, pitted and chopped
- ½ cup feta cheese, crumbled
- 1 teaspoon fresh lemon zest, grated finely

Instructions:

1) In a large baking dish, mix together parsley, 4 garlic cloves, 2 tablespoons of oil, salt and black pepper.
2) Add leg of lamb and coat with parsley mixture generously. Set aside in room temperature.
3) Preheat the oven to 450 degrees F. Grease a shallow roasting pan.
4) In a large skillet, heat remaining oil over medium heat.
5) Add onion and remaining garlic and sauté for about 2-3 minutes.
6) Add kale and cook for about 8-10 minutes.
7) Remove from heat and set aside to cool for at least 10 minutes.
8) Stir in remaining ingredients.
9) Place the leg of lamb onto a smooth surface, cut-side up.
10) Place the kale mixture in the center, leaving 1-inch border from both sides.

11) Roll the short side to seal the stuffing.

12) With a kitchen string tightly, tie the roll at many places.

13) Arrange the roll into prepared roasting pan, seam-side down.

14) Roast for about 15 minutes.

15) Now, reduce the temperature of oven to 350 degrees F.

16) Roast for about 1-1¼ hours.

17) Remove the lamb from oven and set aside for about 10-20 minutes before slicing.

18) With a sharp knife, cut the roll into desired size slices and serve.

Meal Prep Tip: Transfer the lamb slices onto a wire rack to cool completely. With foil pieces, wrap the lamb slices and refrigerate for about 4-5 days. Reheat in the microwave before serving.

Nutrition Information:

Calories per serving: 350; Carbohydrates: 4g; Protein: 44.3g; Fat: 16.5g; Sugar: 0.4g; Sodium: 245mg; Fiber: 0.7g

Day 19

Breakfast: Moist Zucchini Bread

Serves: 12

Cooking Time: 1 hour

Preparation Time: 20 minutes

Ingredients:

- ¾ cup coconut flour
- 1 teaspoon baking powder
- 1½ teaspoons ground cinnamon
- ½ teaspoon salt
- 4 organic eggs (whites and yolks separated)
- 2 organic whole eggs
- ½ cup coconut oil, melted
- ½ cup unsweetened coconut milk
- ½ cup swerve (sugar substitute)
- 1 teaspoon organic vanilla extract
- ¾ cup zucchini, shredded

Instructions:

1) Preheat the oven to 350 degrees F. Grease a 9x5x3-inch a bread loaf pan.
2) In a large bowl, add flour, baking powder, cinnamon and salt and mix well.
3) In a second bowl, add 4 egg whites and beat until fluffy.
4) In a third large bowl, add remaining ingredients except zucchini and beat until well combined.
5) Add egg mixture into the bowl with flour mixture and mix until well combined.
6) Fold in zucchini.
7) Gently, fold in beaten egg whites.
8) Transfer the mixture into prepared loaf pan evenly.

9) Bake for about 1 hour or until a tooth pick inserted in the center comes out clean.

10) Remove the loaf pan from oven and place on a wire rack to cool for at least 10-15 minutes.

11) Carefully, invert the bread onto rack to cool completely.

12) With a sharp knife, cut the bread loaf in desired size slices and serve.

Meal Prep Tip: In a reseal able plastic bag, place the bread slices and seal the bag after squeezing the excess air. Keep the bread away from direct sunlight and preserve in a cool and dry place for about 1-2 days.

Nutrition Information:

Calories per serving: 168; Carbohydrates: 7.1g; Protein: 4.1g; Fat: 14.4g; Sugar: 0.7g; Sodium: 130mg; Fiber: 3.9g

Lunch: Curried Turkey Wraps

Serves: 10

Cooking Time: 15 minutes

Preparation Time: 20 minutes

Ingredients:

- 2 tablespoons unsalted butter
- 1 pound lean ground turkey
- 1 onion, chopped
- 2 garlic cloves, minced
- 1 green bell pepper, seeded and chopped
- 1 cup carrot, peeled and chopped
- ½ cup yellow squash, chopped
- ½ cup zucchini, chopped
- 2 tablespoons low-sodium soy sauce
- ½ teaspoon curry powder
- Freshly ground black pepper, to taste
- 10 large lettuce leaves
- 1½ cups Parmesan cheese, shredded

Instructions:

1) In a large skillet, melt butter over medium heat and cook turkey for about 4-5 minutes, breaking the lumps.
2) Add vegetables and cook for about 4-5 minutes.
3) Add soy sauce, curry powder and black pepper and cook for about 4-5 minutes.
4) Arrange lettuce leaves onto serving plates.
5) Divide the turkey mixture over the leaves evenly.
6) Sprinkle with cheese and serve.

Meal Prep Tip: Remove the turkey mixture from heat and set aside to cool completely. In 10 containers, divide the turkey mixture evenly and refrigerate for about 2 days. Reheat in microwave before serving in lettuce leaves. Top with cheese and serve.

Nutrition Information:

Calories per serving: 136; Carbohydrates: 4.3g; Protein:.12.7g; Fat: 7.8g; Sugar: 2.2g; Sodium: 372mg; Fiber: 0.9g

Dinner: San Franciscan Stew

Serves: 8

Cooking Time: 30 minutes

Preparation Time: 15 minutes

Ingredients:

- 1 tablespoon olive oil
- 1 medium yellow onion, chopped finely
- 1½ teaspoons garlic, minced and divided
- ¼ teaspoon red pepper flakes, crushed
- 1 teaspoon fresh lemon peel, grated finely
- ½ pound plum tomatoes, seeded and chopped finely
- 1 tablespoon sugar-free tomato paste
- 2 cups homemade chicken broth
- 1 pound red snapper fillets, cubed into 1-inch size
- 1 pound raw large shrimp, peeled and deveined
- ½ pound sea scallops
- 1/3 cup fresh parsley, chopped finely
- ½ cup mayonnaise

Instructions:

1) In a large pan, heat oil over medium heat and sauté onion for about 4-6 minutes.
2) Add ½ teaspoon of garlic and red pepper flakes and sauté for about 1 minute.
3) Add lemon peel and tomatoes and cook for about 2-3 minutes, stirring frequently.
4) Add tomato paste, broth and salt and bring to a boil.
5) Reduce the heat to low and simmer, covered for about 10 minutes.
6) Stir in seafood and parsley and simmer, covered for about 8-10 minutes or until desired doneness.
7) Remove from heat and transfer the stew in serving bowls.
8) In a small bowl, mix together remaining garlic and mayonnaise.

9) Top the stew with garlic mayo evenly and serve.

Meal Prep Tip: Transfer the stew into a large bowl and set aside to cool. Divide the mixture into 8 containers evenly. Cover the containers and refrigerate for 1-2 days. Reheat in the microwave before serving.

Nutrition Information:

Calories per serving: 255; Carbohydrates: 8.7g; Protein: 33.5g; Fat: 8.9g; Sugar: 3g; Sodium: 329mg; Fiber: 0.8g

Day 20

Breakfast: Western Omelet

Serves: 4

Cooking Time: 25 minutes

Preparation Time: 15 minutes

Ingredients:

- 6 large organic eggs
- Salt and freshly ground black pepper, to taste
- ½ cup unsweetened coconut milk
- ½ of onion, chopped
- ¼ cup red bell pepper, seeded and chopped
- ¼ cup fresh mushrooms, sliced
- 1 tablespoon chives, minced

Instructions:

1) Preheat the oven to 350 degrees F. Lightly, grease a pie dish.
2) In a bowl, add organic eggs, salt, black pepper and coconut oil. Beat until well combined.
3) In another bowl, mix together onion, bell pepper and mushrooms.
4) Transfer the egg mixture in prepared pie dish evenly.
5) Top with vegetable mixture evenly and sprinkle with chives evenly.
6) Bake for about 20-25 minutes.
7) Cut into desired slices and serve.

Meal Prep Tip: In a resealable plastic bag, place the cooled omelet slices and seal the bag. Refrigerate for about 2-4 days. Reheat in the microwave on High for about 1 minute before serving.

Nutrition Information:

Calories per serving: 185; Carbohydrates: 4.3g; Protein: 10.5g; Fat: 14.7g; Sugar: 2.6g; Sodium: 149mg; Fiber: 1.1g

Lunch: Creamy Comfort Soup

Serves: 4

Cooking Time: 15 minutes

Preparation Time: 15 minutes

Ingredients:

- 4 cups homemade chicken broth
- 20-ounce small broccoli florets
- 12-ounce cheddar cheese, cubed
- Salt and freshly ground black pepper, to taste
- 1 cup heavy cream

Instructions:

1) In a large soup pan, add broth and broccoli and bring to a boil over medium-high heat.
2) Reduce the heat to low and simmer, covered for about 5-7 minutes.
3) Stir in cheese and simmer for about 2-3 minutes, stirring until cheese is melted completely.
4) Stir in black pepper and cream and simmer for about 2 minutes.
5) Serve hot.

Meal Prep Tip: Transfer the soup into a large bowl and set aside to cool. Divide the mixture into 4 containers evenly. Cover the containers and refrigerate for 1-2 days. Reheat in the microwave before serving.

Dinner: Succulent Taco Bake

Serves: 8

Cooking Time: 50 minutes

Preparation Time: 15 minutes

Ingredients for Crust:

- 3 organic eggs
- 4-ounce cream cheese, softened
- ½ teaspoon taco seasoning
- 1/3 cup heavy cream
- 8-ounce cheddar cheese, shredded

Ingredients for Topping:

- 1 pound grass-fed ground beef
- 4-ounce canned chopped green chiles
- ¼ cup sugar-free tomato sauce
- 3 teaspoons taco seasoning
- 8-ounce cheddar cheese, shredded

Instructions:

1) Preheat the oven to 375 degrees F. Lightly. Grease a 13x9-inch baking dish.
2) For crust: in a bowl, add eggs and cream cheese and beat until well combined and smooth.
3) Stir in taco seasoning and heavy cream.
4) Place cheddar cheese in the bottom of prepared baking dish evenly.
5) Spread cream cheese mixture over cheese evenly.
6) Bake for about 25-30 minutes.
7) Remove from oven and set aside for 5 minutes before placing topping.
8) Meanwhile, for topping: heat a large nonstick skillet over medium-high heat and cook beef for about 8-10 minutes.

9) Drain the excess grease from skillet.

10) Stir in remaining ingredients except cheese.

11) Place the beef mixture over crust evenly and sprinkle with cheese evenly.

12) Bake for about 20 minutes or until bubbly.

13) Remove from oven and set aside for about 5 minutes.

14) Cut into desired sized slices and serve.

Meal Prep Tip: Remove the casserole from oven and set aside to cool completely. In 8 containers, divide the casserole pieces evenly and refrigerate for about 2 days. Reheat in microwave before serving.

Nutrition Information:

Calories per serving: 473; Carbohydrates: 11g; Protein:.36.2g; Fat: 31.6g; Sugar: 6g; Sodium: 530mg; Fiber: 4.2g

Day 21

Breakfast: Distinctive Smoothie Bowl

Serves: 3

Preparation Time: 15 minutes

Ingredients:

- 2 cups frozen strawberries
- ½ cup unsweetened almond milk
- ¼ cup fat-free plain Greek yogurt
- 1tablespoons unsweetened whey protein powder
- 2 tablespoons walnuts, chopped

Instructions:

1) In a blender, add frozen strawberries and pulse for about 1 minute.
2) Add almond milk, yogurt and protein powder and pulse until desired consistency is achieved.
3) Transfer the mixture into 2 serving bowls evenly.
4) Serve with the topping of walnuts.

Meal Prep Tip: With a plastic wrap, cover the bowl and refrigerate for about 1-2 days. While serving, top the bowl with a splash of milk and topping ingredients.

Nutrition Information:

Calories per serving: 102; Carbohydrates: 10g; Protein: 7.1g; Fat: 3.9g; Sugar: 6g; Sodium: 63mg; Fiber: 2.5g

Lunch: Wholesome Tuna Burgers

Serves: 2

Cooking Time: 6 minutes

Preparation Time: 15 minutes

Ingredients:

- 1 (15-ounce) can water packed tuna, drained
- ½ celery stalk, chopped
- 2 tablespoons fresh parsley, copped
- 1 teaspoon fresh dill, chopped
- 2 tablespoons walnuts, chopped
- 2 tablespoons mayonnaise
- 1 organic egg, beaten
- 1 tablespoon butter
- ¼ cup cheddar cheese, shredded

Instructions:

1) In a bowl, add all ingredients except butter and cheese and mix until well combined.
2) Make 2 equal sized patties from mixture.
3) In a frying pan, melt butter over medium heat and cook patties for about 2-3 minutes.
4) Carefully, flip the side and top each patty with cheese evenly.
5) Cook for about 2-3 minutes.
6) Serve hot.

Meal Prep Tip: Remove the patties from heat and set aside to cool completely. Store in an airtight container, by placing parchment papers between the burgers to avoid the sticking. These burgers can be stored in the freezer for up to 3 weeks. Before serving, thaw the burgers and then reheat in microwave.

Nutrition Information:

Calories per serving: 644; Carbohydrates: 5.3g; Protein: 65g; Fat: 39.4g; Sugar: 1.4g; Sodium: 377mg; Fiber: 0.8g

Dinner: Veggie Lover's Curry

Serves: 6

Cooking Time: 20 minutes

Preparation Time: 20 minutes

Ingredients:

- 1 medium zucchini, chopped
- 1 medium yellow squash, chopped
- 1 green bell pepper, seeded and cubed
- 1 red bell pepper, seeded and cubed
- 1 onion, sliced thinly
- 2 tablespoons olive oil
- 2 teaspoons curry powder
- Freshly ground black pepper, to taste
- ¼ cup homemade vegetable broth
- ¼ cup fresh cilantro, chopped

Instructions:

1) Preheat the oven to 375 degrees F. Lightly, grease a large baking dish.
2) In a large bowl, add all ingredients except cilantro and mix well.
3) Transfer the vegetables mixture into prepared baking dish.
4) Bake for about 15-20 minutes.
5) Serve immediately and garnish cilantro on top.

Meal Prep Tip: Transfer the curry into a large bowl and set aside to cool. Divide the mixture into 6 containers evenly. Cover the containers and refrigerate for 1-2 days. Reheat in the microwave before serving.

Nutrition Information:

Calories per serving: 74; Carbohydrates: 7.4g; Protein: 1.7g; Fat: 5.1g; Sugar: 4g; Sodium: 41mg; Fiber: 1.9g

Conclusion

Meal prepping has been gaining in popularity. The hectic routines of our daily lives make planning you and your family's meals ahead of time effective and convenient. Saving not only time and money, but also allowing you a medium to have nutritious and tasty food while avoiding fast food, and quick poor choices.

Following a keto plan would be difficult without meal prepping because it follows certain break downs of calories i.e. 5% carbohydrates, 20% proteins and 75% fats. Planning for an entire week relieves you from stressing about what to eat every day.

We hope this guide gives you a healthy start on your way to a successful meal planning.

Made in the USA
Lexington, KY
10 September 2018